Vermont Country Cooking

Vermont Country Cooking

BY
Aristene Pixley

DOVER PUBLICATIONS, INC.
NEW YORK

Published in Canada by General Publishing Company, Ltd., 30 Lesmill Road, Don Mills, Toronto, Ontario. Published in the United Kingdom by Constable and Company, Ltd., 10 Orange Street, London WC2H 7EG.

This Dover edition, first published in 1979, is an unabridged republication of the work originally titled *The Green Mountain Cook Book,* published in 1941 by Stephen Daye Press, Brattleboro, Vermont.

International Standard Book Number: 0-486-23803-2
Library of Congress Catalog Card Number: 78-75140

Manufactured in the United States of America
Dover Publications, Inc.
180 Varick Street
New York, N.Y. 10014

CONTENTS

CONVERSION TABLES FOR FOREIGN EQUIVALENTS

DRY INGREDIENTS

Ounces	Grams	Grams	Ounces	Pounds	Kilograms	Kilograms	Pounds
1 =	28.35	1 =	0.035	1 =	0.454	1 =	2.205
2	56.70	2	0.07	2	0.91	2	4.41
3	85.05	3	0.11	3	1.36	3	6.61
4	113.40	4	0.14	4	1.81	4	8.82
5	141.75	5	0.18	5	2.27	5	11.02
6	170.10	6	0.21	6	2.72	6	13.23
7	198.45	7	0.25	7	3.18	7	15.43
8	226.80	8	0.28	8	3.63	8	17.64
9	255.15	9	0.32	9	4.08	9	19.84
10	283.50	10	0.35	10	4.54	10	22.05
11	311.85	11	0.39	11	4.99	11	24.26
12	340.20	12	0.42	12	5.44	12	26.46
13	368.55	13	0.46	13	5.90	13	28.67
14	396.90	14	0.49	14	6.35	14	30.87
15	425.25	15	0.53	15	6.81	15	33.08
16	453.60	16	0.57				

LIQUID INGREDIENTS

Liquid Ounces	Milliliters	Milliliters	Liquid Ounces	Quarts	Liters	Liters	Quarts
1 =	29.573	1 =	0.034	1 =	0.946	1 =	1.057
2	59.15	2	0.07	2	1.89	2	2.11
3	88.72	3	0.10	3	2.84	3	3.17
4	118.30	4	0.14	4	3.79	4	4.23
5	147.87	5	0.17	5	4.73	5	5.28
6	177.44	6	0.20	6	5.68	6	6.34
7	207.02	7	0.24	7	6.62	7	7.40
8	236.59	8	0.27	8	7.57	8	8.45
9	266.16	9	0.30	9	8.52	9	9.51
10	295.73	10	0.33	10	9.47	10	10.57

Gallons (American)	Liters	Liters	Gallons (American)
1 =	3.785	1 =	0.264
2	7.57	2	0.53
3	11.36	3	0.79
4	15.14	4	1.06
5	18.93	5	1.32
6	22.71	6	1.59
7	26.50	7	1.85
8	30.28	8	2.11
9	34.07	9	2.38
10	37.86	10	2.74

❧ A BRIEF HISTORY of the Spirit prevailing in, and an Introduction to, Vermont Cookery.

LONG ago, when the Thirteen States were still the English Colonies and George the Third of Great Britain was still their sovereign, the cocky state of Vermont was settled and began her career as an independent commonwealth. The country of the Green Mountains was as uncharitable as it was beautiful, and its inhabitants, according to travellers of that day, were a lawless and self-sufficient rabble.

Nevertheless, it was not long before Massachusetts and New York were squabbling over Vermont with main strength. The Vermonters had already become imbued with some of the stubbornness of their rocky fields, and they fought for their integrity tooth and nail. When they found themselves outnumbered they retired to the natural fortress of the Green Mountains, where they remained, unreachable and rooted to the spot, secure for indefinite periods of time. Massachusetts and New York eventually retired in confusion and the Vermonters came down out of the mountains and kept on rooting up stumps.

In the 1770's they became sufficiently conventional to rebel against the Crown, but their fervor was aroused not so much by visions of a united American nation as by a sturdy determination that Vermont should kowtow to nobody, either at home or abroad. They remained stiffnecked even when Ethan Allen was carried in chains to London, and when the Thirteen Colonies had united (with flags waving and drums rolling) in Philadelphia, and not until 1791 did Vermont, with extreme reluctance, abandon her individuality so far as to enter the Union. To the Green Mountain Boys it seemed obvious and without need of saying that no one but themselves could know their needs, and that "the gods of the valleys were not the gods of the hills."

This Vermont self-sufficiency was not by any means pure cussedness. Vermonters knew themselves to be naturally protected—isolated by a great lake, defended by mountains. Native food flourished—deer and wild turkeys in the forests, bass and pickerel in the lakes, trout in the streams. In the spring they tapped the sugar maple, and in the fall their harvest of staple foods was abundant. They raised Morgan horses, and sheep grazed on the side hills. Vermont could support herself and produce what she needed—men, beasts, and food.

Now, after a century or more, Vermont has softened a little. Civilization and modern progress have broken down frontiers against which the powder of King George was powerless, and have drawn nearer to the farmer on his side hill, forcing him to come down into the valley and see his neighbors. Rocky uphill roads have not discouraged tourists, nor sagging roofs and knotted orchards the buyers of abandoned farms. But the sturdy individuality of Vermont has not yet become blurred—on the back roads and hill farms she is still untamed and beautiful—and she still does her own cooking!

Vermonters are generally too reticent to become famous. Some few have—Calvin Coolidge, John Dewey, John L. Sullivan, Stuart Sherman, and Admiral Dewey for example. And one whose name is especially appropriate to this book—Louis Sherry. Whether he was inspired by his native soil or by the skyline of New York we do not know; but the foods grown in Vermont fields and woods, and cooked, to this day, in certain kitchens according to certain recipes, are not unworthy of his gifts.

One hundred, or even fifty, years ago this cooking of

food was an act that took half a woman's life. The kitchen
was the arena of the house. The men of the family might
"set" there in the evening, but it was the woman's battle-
field and her sanctuary, and she ran two miles before
breakfast across its floors. There was a fireplace, for boiling and roasting, a wood stove, a pastry table, a milk-room,
a smoke-house, a cellar—and the extent of this cooking
territory was matched only by the scope and volume of the
old handwritten cookbooks. A modern housewife would
faint at the thought of concocting some of the recipes
within the extreme limits of the modern kitchen and of the
time she allots herself for culinary activities. Others,
family standbys handed down from mother to daughter,
are simple and sufficiently economical and even a hole-in-
the-wall kitchenette would accommodate them. After all,
not much space is required to make honey or maple sugar
pudding sauce; and a Vermont turkey needs only one oven.

Some of the recipes gathered in this book are local—but
they belong as much to the whole of Vermont as to Lake
Memphremagog or Mount Mansfield. Many are national,
but modulated, made different by an original flavor, or
condiment, or method of cooking. The unexpected quality
in these recipes is their delicacy and richness. The pleas-
ures of the table were not forbidden to our stern puritani-
cal forefathers. There is an exotic use of cream and eggs
which, after all, is the only way to make things delicious.

And they had their native drinks too, these rockbound Vermonters. Most cellars were well stocked with cider and there was metheglin or mead, potent and wonderfully good, made from honey.

In this book we have tried to temper our enthusiasm with a little native Vermont self-control. These recipes will not take your whole life and a kitchen range to perfect, nor must you tap your own maples and feed your own hens to try them out and keep within your budget. For, wherever these foods are cooked, you may be sure that they were flavored in Vermont.

ANY NATIVE Vermonter must have pleasant memories of cold winter nights cheered by "bean porridge hot" for supper, accompanied by Montpelier crackers — large, double, and hearty. This, a little dressed up, is the recipe:

Bean Soup

Soak the beans over night. Add to them a few cloves and pepper corns, salt, two tablespoons of chopped onion. Pour over them cold water to cover and simmer till beans are soft, adding water if needed. Strain and add stock or water to make the consistency of a thick cream. Mash the yolk of a hard-boiled egg. Add this to a tablespoon each of flour and butter, blended. Add to soup and cook five minutes. Reduce with water if necessary.

Beet Soup

Chop six cooked beets while hot, and simmer in a quart of milk till pulpy. Strain, season, thicken slightly and serve with whipped cream.

Potato Soup

Cut the potatoes in thin slices or dice, and cook in just enough salted water to boil down. When soft, season and add half cream and half milk, butter and a small amount of minced onion. Or, place a few rings of onion (uncooked) in the bottom of each soup plate.

Vegetable Soup

Chop uncooked vegetables—cabbage, potatoes, carrots, beets and one or two onions. Cook slowly in salted water, adding a small amount of sage and minced ham for seasoning.

Parsnip Chowder

Chop a small onion fine and fry it in two tablespoons of finely chopped salt pork or bacon. Add this to two cups of diced parsnips and one of potatoes, season with salt and pepper. Pour over this two cups of boiling water and cook till soft. Add one quart of milk, one-half cup of butter, one-half cup of cracker crumbs and a tablespoon of minced parsley or mint.

Mushroom Soup

Take one and a half cups of mushrooms cut into small pieces, and cook in two tablespoons of melted butter till tender but not brown. Remove the mushrooms and brown a tablespoon of flour in the butter. Meanwhile, cook another cup and a half of mushrooms, also cut small, in a pint of milk and a half pint of cream. Cook till the cream is well flavored. Remove the mushrooms from the cream and add it slowly to the browned flour. Return to a double boiler, add all the mushrooms and blend well, then strain.

Onion Soup

Slice three large white onions and fry brown in butter, adding two tablespoons flour. Add six cups beef stock, one-half teaspoon each salt and celery salt, one-eighth teaspoon pepper and a dash of cayenne. Boil till onions are very soft. Put in each soup plate a slice of thin toast sprinkled with grated cheese, and pour soup over it.

Onion Cream Soup

Blend in a saucepan four level tablespoons flour and four of butter, with a teaspoon of salt and one-eighth teaspoon of pepper. Add one quart of rich milk, very hot, and thicken. Cook separately enough onions to make two cups when soft and chopped. Add to milk any water left from cooking.

Sweet Potato Soup

Take two cups of cooked sweet potatoes, riced, and one-half cup of cooked rice, mix and put through the ricer together. Add one quart of hot milk slowly and put in double boiler. Brown separately two tablespoons flour, mixed with three of butter or bacon fat. When smooth, add to the soup mixture gradually. Season with salt and a dash of cinnamon or cloves.

Split Pea Soup

Soak half a package of split peas over night in cold water. Add a large slice of salt pork or three strips of bacon, a level teaspoon of salt, one-fourth teaspoon of celery salt and a half dozen each pepper corns and cloves. Brown in butter a large onion sliced, and add. Pour over six cups of water, simmer till peas are tender, adding water as necessary, and strain.

A FAVORITE Vermont dish is salt salmon with cream, served with baked potatoes. Try to find it in New York markets or restaurants! Plenty that is smoked in delicatessens, but not the dried salted salmon, which is prepared as follows:

Salt Salmon with Cream

Soak a piece of salt salmon over night in enough sour milk to cover. Rinse carefully, place in cold water to cover and let it come to a boil slowly. Take salmon from the water, remove any skin or bones, place on platter and pour hot cream and melted butter over it.

Creamed Codfish

Freshen flaked salt codfish by placing in a frying pan with cold water, and letting it come to a boil. Pour off the water, add to the codfish a rich cream sauce, and just before serving stir in a raw egg.

Baked Salmon

Mix a can of salmon with a cup of hot cream, a tablespoon of butter, and a beaten egg. Season, put in a baking-dish, cover with hot mashed potato and bake slowly for twenty minutes.

Baked Fish with Nuts

Cream two tablespoons of butter with the same amount of flour, then add salt, pepper, a dash of cayenne and a pint of hot milk. When thick, stir in a cup of flaked fish, a cup of finely chopped or ground peanuts, and three hard-boiled eggs chopped fine. Put in a baking-dish, cover with cracker crumbs and bake lightly.

Fish with Rice

Boil two cups of rice, drain well and mix in two chopped hard-boiled eggs, two cups of any cold fish, flaked, a tablespoon of butter, a tablespoon of cream, half a teaspoon of salt and a little nutmeg. Mix thoroughly and heat for ten minutes. Serve with piccalilli.

Trout Fried

Wash and dry, sprinkle with salt and roll in a mixture of flour and cornmeal. Fry in butter, turning carefully so as not to break. Garnish with water cress.

Trout Baked

Place the trout in a buttered baking-pan, salt and cover completely with cream. Bake till the cream is brown, and serve in the dish in which the fish is baked.

Perch Fried

Prepare and fry in the same way as trout.   If the fish are quite small, use oatmeal in the place of cornmeal.   Serve with lemon.

Pickerel Baked

Cut head and tail from pickerel, wipe clean and dry and rub with salt and butter.   Stuff with a dressing of bread crumbs, moistened with milk and seasoned with salt, pepper and sage. Put small amount of butter and water in baking-pan and baste several times while baking.

Bass Baked

Proceed as with pickerel above, using a rather less highly seasoned dressing.

Frogs' Legs

Lay frogs' legs in a dish, cover with oil, salt, pepper and a little lemon juice, and leave for a half hour.   Rub the broiler with an onion.   Broil five or six minutes on each side, pour melted butter over them and serve.   If fried in butter, a little less time will be required.

Oyster Pie

Line a baking-dish with a meat-pie pastry and fill with layers of oysters, pouring over them the oyster liquor and seasoning with salt and pepper.   Dot with butter and sprinkle a little flour over them, put on a top layer of pastry and bake rather slowly, after the pastry has risen in a hot oven.   An incision should be made in the top pastry for the escape of steam.   Half a cup of cream may be poured into the pie before serving, lifting the top carefully.

Quick Oysters

Place a pint of oysters in a pan with a small piece of butter, salt and pepper. Have ready a cup of finely rolled cracker crumbs. When the oysters begin to curl, stir in the cracker crumbs till they absorb the juice. Stir in a well-beaten egg, cooking a minute more.

Scalloped Oysters

Brown one cup of cracker crumbs in one-half cup of butter. Butter a baking-dish, put a layer of crumbs in the bottom, then half a pint of oysters and season with salt and pepper. Put over them another layer of cracker crumbs, another half pint of oysters and more seasoning. Mix a beaten egg with a cup of milk and pour over, then add a top layer of crumbs. Bake in moderate oven.

MEATS

Not so many years ago, in Vermont, every well-stocked cellar had—in addition to winter vegetables, a swinging-shelf of jellies and preserves, barrels of apples and cider—a barrel of pork in brine. Fried salt pork was perhaps as characteristic of Vermont cookery as the elaborately roasted Vermont turkey itself. Sliced thin, fried till crisp, and served with baked potatoes and "milk gravy" made in the pan in which the pork was fried, it is a dish not to be disdained. As for the turkey:

Vermont Turkey Roasted

Rub the turkey with salt, then with a mixture of one-third cup of butter and one-fourth cup of flour. Stuff with a dressing of bread crumbs moistened with milk and melted butter, and well seasoned with salt, pepper and sage. Dredge the bottom of the roasting-pan with flour, and start the roasting in a hot oven. When the flour begins to brown, reduce the heat. Baste with the fat in the pan to which two cups of boiling water have been added.   Cook a ten-pound turkey about three hours, basting every fifteen minutes and adding butter and boiling water to the mixture in the pan as needed.   Turn the turkey frequently.

Vermont Chicken Pie

Make a batter of two cups of flour, five teaspoons of baking-powder, one teaspoon of salt, one cup of milk and five table-spoons of shortening—half butter and half chicken fat.   Add more milk if the batter seems too thick.   This makes a crust for two small chickens.   Cook the chickens as for fricassee, place in baking pan, cover with plenty of gravy made from the chicken stock, season and dot with butter, and place over this the batter, with a cup in the center to allow steam to escape.

Smothered Chicken

Put into a roasting-pan with a tightly fitting cover two cups of stock (this may be made from bouillon cubes—one cube to each cup of boiling water) ; next the gizzard, heart and liver of the chicken.   Split the chicken, place in the pan over the giblets, cover tightly and roast.   When done, remove the chicken to a platter, mash the giblets, add a cup of cream, thicken and season. Have baking-powder biscuits ready, split and place around the chicken on the platter and cover with the gravy.

Chicken Shortcake

Bake a shortcake as for fruit, split and butter.   Have ready cold chicken, cut in small slices.   Fill the bottom layer and spread with mayonnaise.   Place on the top half peas and string beans mixed with mayonnaise.   Serve with the shortcake as hot as possible.   Or use creamed chicken on the bottom layer and creamed vegetables on the top, instead. Mushrooms and peas are a good combination.

Chicken and Rice

Cook half a cup of rice in one and one-half cups of milk. Add salt, a tablespoon of butter and one egg. Line cups with this. Chop cooked chicken, season with salt and pepper and moisten with milk or gravy, and add two tablespoons of chopped pimentos. Fill the cups, cover with rice and bake in a pan of water for twenty minutes. Serve with cream sauce, or garnish with cress and hard-boiled eggs.

Ham Slices Baked

Lay thin slices of ham in a baking-dish and cover with a mixture of one-half cup of water, one tablespoon of dry mustard, two tablespoons of sugar and three tablespoons of vinegar. Cook in a moderate oven and baste frequently, adding more water and vinegar if required.

Ham Baked with Cider

Wash the ham in hot water. Soak over night in cold water. Rinse it off, then place in cold water and bring slowly to the boiling point; add bay leaf, cloves and allspice, and simmer till tender. Cool, remove skin, then soak over night in one and one-half quarts of cider. Dry, and stick cloves over surface. Make a mixture of bread crumbs and a cup of maple sugar. Brush the ham with beaten egg, then cover it with the mixture. Place in a baking-pan, pour the cider carefully over it and baste. Bake till brown.

Ham Loaf

Soak a tablespoon of gelatine in one-fourth cup of cold water, and dissolve in three-fourths cup of hot stock. Strain this over one cup of finely minced ham, season with salt and pepper, set in a pan of cold water and stir constantly till it begins to set. Have ready one cup of cream beaten stiff, fold this into the ham mixture and place on ice for several hours.

Slow Steak

Use top round steak, and pound thoroughly with edge of thick plate. Brown in frying-pan with butter, season, cover with hot water and simmer for an hour as slowly as possible.

Steak with Dressing

Take a pound and a half of top round steak or sirloin, spread with butter and season. The steak should be about half an inch thick. Spread with a dressing made of bread crumbs moistened with stock, and well seasoned with salt, pepper and sage, roll and tie to hold in shape. Bake till tender, and cut across the roll to serve.

Lamb Stew

Slice two or three onions and cut up potatoes and carrots. Brown in butter for a few minutes. Put pieces of lamb cut for a stew in cold water, let it come to a boil and simmer slowly for half an hour. Add the vegetables, and continue cooking slowly. Fifteen minutes before ready, drop in dumplings No. 2, cover tightly and cook for that period.

Veal Cutlets

Remove all fat and gristle from a pound of veal, and cut in thin slices. Beat an egg lightly with a pinch of salt, dip the pieces of meat into this and roll in sifted bread crumbs. Put a tablespoon of butter into the frying-pan, and when very hot add the meat. Fry a golden brown, season and serve with lemon or a piccalilli relish.

Veal Special

Place a pound and a half of veal in boiling water to cover, and simmer for an hour and a half to two hours. Add water as necessary. To the small amount remaining add a cup of sour cream, season well, simmer for a few minutes more and serve.

Pork Chops

Put a piece of bacon into the frying-pan and, when very hot, sear six pork chops, both sides. Add quickly six medium-sized potatoes, peeled and cut in very thin slices, arrange over the meat, cover closely and cook slowly.

Pork Tenderloins

Wipe carefully and place in a baking-pan. Brown the tenderloins quickly. Remove and sprinkle with salt, pepper and sage, and dot with butter. Bake forty-five minutes, basting occasionally.

Braised Liver

Put one cup of celery, cut in small pieces, in the bottom of a baking-dish. Place over this three-fourths of a pound of liver, and add butter and seasoning. Add three tablespoons of water, cover and bake half to three-quarters of an hour. Cook four each small onions and carrots, and add to the meat. Add a cup of stock, thickened. Cook for a few minutes more and serve.

Calves' Liver Special

Cut two pounds of liver in small pieces, and place in a frying-pan with a tablespoon of butter and a chopped onion. Season well with salt and pepper and cook five minutes. Then add three tablespoons of sherry or Madeira and half a dozen chopped mushrooms, and cook till tender.

Baked Sausage

Place small cakes of sausage in a large baking-pan, pour over them a Yorkshire pudding batter, and bake about thirty minutes. Use a large enough pan so that the batter will be very thin. Make the batter with one cup of flour, one-half teaspoon of salt, two well-beaten eggs and one cup of milk.

Meat Souffle

Mix one tablespoon of butter with a heaping tablespoon of flour, and salt and pepper. Cook with a cup of milk till thick. Add one cup of cold meat, chopped fine, a minced onion, the yolks of two eggs and half a level teaspoon of baking powder. Allow it to cool, then add the beaten whites of the eggs and bake twenty minutes. Salmon or halibut is suggested in the place of meat, and lobster or crab meat is excellent.

New England Boiled Dinner

Place several pounds of corned beef—brisket—in cold water and boil for fifteen minutes. Skim carefully. Then simmer till tender. During the last hour of cooking add the various vegetables—carrots, potatoes and turnips cut in rather large pieces, cabbage cut in quarters and sliced onions. Season well.

CHEESE

THE MARKETS are now full of cheese of every variety, foreign and domestic, and most of them excellent. But when it comes to cooking, the old standard country cheese —"store cheese"—at the right state of ripeness, neither too young nor too old, is the best. It melts easily and has strength and flavor. Here is a simple and very good old recipe:

Cheese Puffs

Beat together an egg that has been lightly whipped, two cups of mashed potato, two tablespoons of butter, two tablespoons of grated cheese, with salt and pepper. Form into cakes about three inches across and half an inch thick and bake in a hot oven.

Cheese Pie

Cut two-thirds of a small loaf of bread in half slices. Alternate in a baking-dish with layers of soft, rather mild cheese in thin slices. Sprinkle with salt, pepper and nutmeg. Over this pour two eggs beaten with a cup of milk. Bake thirty minutes.

Cheese Croquettes

Cut a pound of country cheese in small pieces. Have ready a

cup of hot cream sauce in a saucepan. Add the cheese with the
yolks of two eggs, beaten and diluted with a little cream. Stir
over the fire till the cheese is well melted. Season with salt,
pepper, cayenne and a little nutmeg. Place the mixture on ice
till cold, then form into croquettes. Roll in fine bread crumbs,
dip in egg, roll in crumbs again and fry in deep fat.

Cheese with Nuts

Place layers of chopped walnuts in a baking-dish, alternating
with layers of grated cheese and bread crumbs. Season with butter, salt and pepper and moisten with hot water. Bake twenty
minutes.

Cold Rabbit

Melt a tablespoon of butter in a saucepan, add a pound of
cheese broken into small pieces and, when melted, pour in half
a cup of ale or milk. Mix thoroughly, add a teaspoon of mixed
mustard, a dash of cayenne, a tablespoon of any sharp sauce and,
lastly, three well-beaten egg yolks. Cook till it thickens, in a
double boiler, and turn into a mold to chill.

Cheese Souffle

To a tablespoon of melted butter in a hot saucepan, add three
cups of cheese, broken very fine. Season with a salt-spoon each
of salt, mustard and paprika, and a dash of cayenne. Dissolve
half a level teaspoon of soda in half a cup of water, and add
this to the cheese. Beat the yolks of two eggs with a tablespoon
of cold water and stir in. When smooth and creamy, add a teaspoon each of lemon juice and Worcestershire sauce, and stir in

quickly the whites of the eggs, well beaten. Bake and serve immediately.

Cheese and Apple

Take half a pound of soft country cheese and a third as much butter. Rub together till well blended, adding a tablespoon of cognac or sherry. Spread on slices of apple.

EGGS

OF COURSE, the typical egg dish for the state of Vermont, as for every other state in the Union, is ham and eggs. But the methods of cooking eggs are practically unlimited, and the following is an old-time recipe which is unusual and extremely good:

Eggs Fairlee

Slice three or four onions and fry in butter. Drain them and place in the bottom of a dish for serving. Boil very hard—fifteen minutes—eight eggs. Slice six of them, place them on the onions and cover the dish to keep hot. Mash the yolks of the two remaining eggs, mix with cream, a little grated nutmeg or any piquant seasoning. Chop the two whites and stir into the cream mixture. Let it just come to a boil, pour over the eggs and onions and serve.

Eggs with Sausage

Break up two cakes of sausage meat and cook for five minutes.

Make a plain omelet by beating the yolks of six eggs, adding a teaspoon of water for each egg. Season and fold in the stiffly beaten whites. Beat thoroughly and cook at once. When brown, fold one edge a third over, cover with the hot sausage and fold over the other third. Place the omelet in a hot oven a minute before serving.

Omelet Celestial

Break four eggs in a bowl and beat just enough to mix the whites and yolks. Add a tablespoon each of powdered sugar and cream, and a little butter. Put a tablespoon of melted butter in a saucepan, add the eggs and, when set, add three tablespoons of strawberry or other jam. Fold and dust with powdered sugar.

Quick Omelet

Beat the yolks of four eggs, add a teaspoon of sugar, a little salt and pepper and two teaspoons of cream. Pour in pan and when just about to cook through, whisk over the beaten whites and turn carefully.

Eggs Baked

Butter fireproof cups or muffin rings, and put two tablespoons of cream in each. Break an egg in each and dust with salt and pepper. Peas, bits of asparagus, mushrooms or any cooked, left-over vegetable may be placed on the eggs, or they may be covered with grated cheese. Then sprinkle with cracker crumbs and bake till the eggs are set.

Eggs with Asparagus

Cover the bottom of a baking-dish with cooked asparagus tips, fresh or canned. Poach eggs and lay on the asparagus, then pour over them a thin cream sauce seasoned with salt, pepper and curry powder. Bake three or four minutes.

Eggs with Potato

Beat together two cups of hot mashed potato, three tablespoons of butter, half a cup of cream or rich milk, a tablespoon of chopped mint, salt and pepper. Put in baking-dish, make six indentations and break an egg in each. Dot with butter and bake till eggs are set.

Creamed Eggs

Melt butter in a saucepan, and add half a teaspoon each of salt, pepper, tobasco sauce and nutmeg. Pour in a sufficient quantity of cream, let it boil up and poach the eggs in this, pouring what is left when they are cooked over them.

Eggs and Cheese

Poach three eggs in half a pint of rich cream. Remove the eggs and place on slices of buttered toast which have been sprinkled with minced ham. Add two tablespoons of grated country cheese to the cream, with seasoning. Simmer till the cheese is melted, then pour mixture over the eggs.

Perhaps the earliest dish in Vermont cookery is what is known as hasty pudding, or cornmeal mush. It is eaten hot for supper. For breakfast the next morning, sliced and fried in butter until the outside is crisp, and served with maple syrup, it can compete with waffles and corn syrup any time. This is how it is prepared:

Hasty Pudding

To a pint of boiling water, stir in a cup of cornmeal and a tablespoon of flour mixed with cold water. Add salt and stir well, being careful there are no lumps. Cook slowly for about ten minutes. To be eaten hot in milk. If enough is cooked for a breakfast dish, it should be placed while hot in a buttered mold. When ready to use, cut in slices and fry till brown and crisp on both sides, then serve with maple syrup.

Cornmeal Souffle

Scald a pint of rich milk, and add a cup of sifted cornmeal and a teaspoon of salt. Stir till smooth. Add one teaspoon of baking powder. Stir in thoroughly four well-beaten egg yolks, and fold in the beaten whites. Bake till firm and brown.

Cornmeal with Cheese

Make mush by stirring one cup of cornmeal into two cups of milk, and adding to two cups of boiling salted water. Stir till thick, and add two heaping tablespoons of grated cheese and one of butter. Cool in small molds, turn out on a baking-dish, sprinkle with grated cheese and baste with melted butter. Brown in the oven, and serve as a garnish for meat or fish.

Cornmeal Griddle Cakes

Add a teaspoon of soda to one and one-half cups of sour milk. Add one beaten egg, one tablespoon of sugar, one teaspoon of salt, half a cup of flour, and meal to make a thick batter. Serve with maple syrup.

Rice with Cheese

Cook rice very tender in salted water. Make a rich cream sauce, stir in a generous amount of grated cheese, with two tablespoons chopped mint or sorrel. Pour over the rice and serve.

Macaroni Champlain

Boil three-fourths of a pound of macaroni in two quarts of salted water for half an hour. Put a large cup of beef stock in a saucepan, add three or four tomatoes, cut up, half a dozen medium-sized onions, sliced, a large piece of butter and salt and pepper. To this add three or four cakes of sausage, broken up, and cook all together while the macaroni is cooking. Drain the macaroni, and place in a deep buttered baking-dish. Pour the mixture over it and blend well. Put bits of butter on the top and bake for half an hour. Sprinkle a large cup of grated cheese over it just before taking from oven.

Macaroni Omelet

Cut two cups of cold cooked macaroni very fine. In a large bowl beat four eggs with salt and a tablespoon of minced parsley, then stir in the macaroni and beat together. Heat a tablespoon of butter in a saucepan, pour in the mixture, brown on one side and turn out on a plate. Add more butter to the saucepan, and brown the macaroni on the other side. When the eggs are cooked through, slip upon a hot platter and serve with more parsley.

Macaroni Ring

Stir a quarter cup of melted butter with three cups of cooked macaroni, cut fine. Add the beaten yolks of three eggs, and then the stiffly beaten whites. Bake for twenty minutes in a ring mold set in a pan of water. Turn the mold on a hot platter and use as a border for any meat or fish preparation made with a sauce.

VEGETABLES

THIS IS certainly a most typical Vermont dish, one that is always popular, simple though it seems:

Red Flannel Hash

Chop equal parts of potatoes and beets, cooked. Place in a frying-pan two tablespoons of bacon fat or butter and add the vegetables, seasoning well with salt and pepper. Moisten with hot water and cook slowly, covered, then brown quickly and just before taking up, add a tablespoon of cream and a little more butter. A cup of chopped meat may be added to the p tatoes and beets if desired.

Baked Beans Vermont

Wash a pint of beans and soak them over night. The next day put in boiling water and cook for an hour and a half. Wash and heat half a pound of fat salt pork. Place it in the bean pot. Drain the beans and pour cold water over them. Place them in the bean pot, covering the pork. Mix half a cup of molasses, three teaspoons of salt, three tablespoons of sugar and two teaspoons of dry mustard. Add to this enough boiling water so that the mixture will cover the beans. Bake six to seven hours in a very slow oven, adding more water if necessary.

Baked Vegetable Hash

Put through the meat grinder, uncooked, equal parts of potatoes, beets, carrots and cabbage, and one or two onions. Add
to the mixture any vegetable juice which may drip from the
grinder and enough milk to moisten well, season and dot the top
generously with butter. Bake for about forty-five minutes, or till
well cooked.

Potatoes Champlain

Peel potatoes and cut a small cavity in each. Place in this a
very small onion. Roll in flour, salt and place in buttered pan.
When they start to brown in the oven, baste with butter or bacon
fat melted in a cup of hot water. Garnish with cress or mint.

Baked Potatoes Special

Bake large potatoes and, when just done, cut a small piece of
the skin from the top of each. Scoop out most of the inside, mix
with cream, butter, pepper and salt and replace in the skins, leav-
ing, however, in each potato a cavity large enough to bake an
egg. Replace and bake till the eggs are set.

Potatoes with Onions

Cut four potatoes in thin slices. Put two tablespoons of butter
in a saucepan with a dozen little onions, cut small. Heat the
onions in the butter to a golden brown, add the potatoes, a teaspoon of chopped parsley, salt, pepper and a squeeze of lemon.
Cook, stirring constantly, for about eight minutes.

Creamed Potatoes (1)

Chop cold cooked potatoes fine and season well with salt and pepper. Put them in a frying-pan with a large tablespoon of butter and milk to cover. Cook them very slowly, covered, till the milk is absorbed. Uncover and brown well, stirring as they brown. Just before taking from the fire, add enough thick cream to make them of the right consistency.

Creamed Potatoes (2)

Boil potatoes, cool and cut in thin slices. Cover with cream and simmer till the cream begins to thicken. Add pepper, salt, a little mace and a few drops of lemon juice.

Baked Brown Potatoes

Boil and mash a dozen small potatoes. Beat into them while hot a teaspoon of onion juice, salt, pepper, half a cup of cream and a tablespoon of butter. Blend till smooth and creamy, place in a buttered cake tin and bake brown in a hot oven.

Sweet Potato Fluff

Mix three cups of mashed sweet potatoes with one cup of pineapple juice, two teaspoons salt, three tablespoons butter and three-fourths of a cup of shredded pineapple in the order named. Bake till brown.

Sweet Potato Special

Cook large sweet potatoes and cut them in slices half an inch thick. Place in a baking-dish and on each slice place slices of bananas. Pour maple syrup over the whole, and bake, basting often.

Asparagus with Sauce

Remove the tough ends of two pounds of fresh asparagus, and wash. Cook till tender. Cream together two tablespoons of butter, two egg yolks and one-fourth teaspoon of salt. Add a teaspoon each of lemon juice and grated orange peel. Cook the sauce over a pan of hot water till it thickens, then add five table-spoons of orange juice, blend and pour over asparagus, or serve separately.

Mushrooms and Asparagus

Peel a pound of mushrooms, discard stems and fry in butter till brown. Add a pint of cream with a little flour to thicken. Let it come to a boil, then add a can of asparagus tips, with salt, pepper and celery salt. Heat well but do not boil, and serve on hot buttered toast.

Roasted Mushrooms

Prepare one and one-half pounds large mushrooms. Chop fine one medium-sized onion and the mushroom stems, season and place in the cups of the mushroom tops, together with a piece of butter in each. Place in a baking-dish and add a small amount of milk, not enough to run into the tops. Bake thirty minutes. Pour over the mushrooms the juice slightly thickened.

Brussels Sprouts with Chestnuts

Let the sprouts stand in salted water for an hour, then boil uncovered. Slash the shells of an equal quantity of chestnuts, bake for five minutes, then boil till tender. Season the sprouts, add cream and butter and mix with the chestnuts.

Quick Cabbage

Cook a quart of cabbage which has been shredded fine in about two cups of boiling milk for five or six minutes. Make a sauce with cream, flour, salt and pepper, and stir into the boiling cabbage. Cook for two or three minutes more.

String Beans Vermont

Break the beans in small pieces and boil in slightly salted water. To a quart and a half of beans add one small onion sliced. When tender, season with salt, pepper and butter, stir in a large potato, mashed, and half a cup of hot sweet cream.

Puff Balls

These are rare but a great delicacy. Slice the balls about one-third of an inch thick, fry carefully at once in butter, season with salt, and serve with pieces of lemon.

Squash

Select a squash that is hard and solid, cut the shell into sections and bake till well done. Remove the squash from the shell, season with salt and pepper and a generous amount of butter.

Parsnips with Cheese

Boil parsnips till soft, and mash them. Add salt, grated country cheese and butter. Add sufficient milk, or half milk and half cream, to make a smooth, creamy mixture. Place in a baking-dish, cover with bread crumbs, dot the top with butter and bake brown.

Greens

The best Spring greens are cowslip, beet and dandelion. Wash the greens thoroughly and scrape the roots. Drain and cook for an hour in a small quantity of boiling salted water. Season, and serve with vinegar.

Corn with Ham

Place half a can of corn in a buttered baking-dish, and over it a quarter cup of cracker crumbs and a cup of minced boiled ham. Season and add butter, then the rest of the corn, another quarter cup of crumbs, and more butter and seasoning. Pour over about a cup of milk, enough to cover, and bake for half an hour.

Scalloped Tomatoes

Drain a can of tomatoes and cut enough stale bread into small cubes to make a quart. Place the bread in the oven and let it brown. Put a layer of the bread in a baking-dish, then tomatoes and seasoning. Alternate with the bread and tomatoes, placing the bread cubes on top and pouring over them melted butter. Bake ten minutes.

Cauliflower with Cheese

Break up a head of cauliflower, and let it stand for a time in cold salted water. Boil with the saucepan uncovered. Place in a buttered baking-dish, and cover with a cream sauce into which has been stirred a liberal quantity of grated country cheese and half a teaspoon of caraway seeds.

Stewed Cucumbers

Peel large cucumbers, and quarter them lengthwise. Boil them about twenty-five minutes in salted water. Place on toast. Put a tablespoon of butter in a pan and blend with a tablespoon of flour. Add a cup of boiling water, simmer for a few moments, then another tablespoon of butter, salt and pepper and two tablespoons of lemon juice. Pour over the cucumbers and serve.

Baked Onions

Boil six medium-sized onions till tender, drain and place in a shallow baking-dish. Pour over sufficient milk to cover—about one cup—into which has been stirred a tablespoon of tapioca. Add a tablespoon of butter, half a teaspoon of salt and a little pepper. Just before taking from oven, sprinkle well with grated cheese. It should bake till the tapioca is set.

Gilfeather Turnips

Pare Gilfeather Turnips and cut into small cubes. Soak in ice-cold water for an hour or more. Boil in salted water that more than covers. Cook, with top of kettle off, for fifteen to twenty minutes. When tender, season with butter, salt and pepper, and serve.

SALADS

IN A land of mountains and hills, with brooks everywhere, is found the best of all salads—water cress. There is nothing to compare with it in crispness and tang. It should be dressed with the simplest French dressing—oil, tarragon vinegar, salt and pepper. Other simple salads are:

Vegetable Salad

Cut four cooked carrots and four cooked potatoes in thin slices and add a cup of peas. Add to this a small raw onion, sliced thin, a little celery and parsley, minced, and mix well with French dressing.

Orange Salad

To crisp lettuce hearts add sections of a seedless orange, and dress thoroughly with a French dressing, using tarragon vinegar and a few grains of cayenne.

Cabbage Salad

Chop the cabbage very fine and mix with crushed pineapple. Mix with mayonnaise thinned with a little cream and having a dash of cayenne added.

Carrot Salad

Grate raw carrots and mix with a well-flavored apple, chopped, using a thin mayonnaise into which has been stirred a small amount of mint or sorrel, minced.

Potato Salad

Make the usual potato salad with a thin mayonnaise dressing, and add two or three nasturtium leaves, minced, and two of the blossoms, broken in small pieces.

Aspic Special

Soak two tablespoons of gelatine in one cup of water. In two cups of water simmer one slice of onion, a tablespoon of chopped carrots, a clove, a bay leaf and a salt spoon each of pepper and celery salt. After ten minutes, strain, mix with the gelatine and add half a teaspoon of beef extract, the juice of half a lemon and half a teaspoon of salt. Place on ice. Excellent for meat or vegetables.

Quick Mayonnaise

Put into a bowl that has been chilled three tablespoons of oil, the yolk of a very fresh egg, one tablespoon of lemon juice or tarragon vinegar, salt and pepper. Have all the ingredients very cold, and beat steadily with an egg-beater.

French Dressing

To three tablespoons of oil add from a teaspoon to a table-spoon of vinegar, depending upon the strength, salt and pepper. Tarragon vinegar gives the best flavor. Or use cider vinegar in which a few caraway seeds have been placed.

SAUCES

With maple sugar in every form one of the chief products of the state, it is natural that it should be used freely in cooking, and its delicious and distinctive flavor improves many varieties of food. It is used in canning and pickling, in pies, cakes and puddings, and here is an excellent pudding sauce with a maple syrup foundation:

Maple Syrup Sauce

Boil three-fourths of a cup of maple syrup with half a cup of water till it threads. Add it slowly to the stiffly whipped whites of two eggs, half a cup of cream and a teaspoon of lemon juice, beating all the while with an egg-beater.

Maple Sugar Sauce (1)

Grate half a pound of maple sugar into a cup of cream or milk, and let it boil very slowly for a few minutes, stirring occasionally.

Maple Sugar Sauce (2)

Mix two cups of maple sugar with two well-beaten eggs, the

juice of two lemons and a dessertspoon of butter. Cook in a double boiler for twenty minutes.

Hard Sauce (1)

Cream four tablespoons of butter with a cup of sugar, having scalded the bowl and fork. Add the white of an egg, beaten dry, and the juice of a lemon.

Hard Sauce (2)

Take a teaspoon of butter and two tablespoons of milk, add a little vanilla and thicken to the right consistency with powdered sugar, stirring well.

Old-Fashioned Sauce

To a cup of cream add two tablespoons of maple sugar, a pinch of salt, and grated nutmeg to flavor.

Plum Pudding Sauce

Cream half a cup of butter and a cup of powdered sugar. Add a teaspoon of vanilla and a wine glass of sherry. Beat well, and just before serving stir in a cup of boiling water and the stiffly beaten white of an egg. Beat till it foams.

Marmalade Sauce

Mix four tablespoons of orange or grape fruit marmalade, a wine glass of sherry, the juice of a lemon, the juice of an orange and three tablespoons of sugar. Add the whites of two eggs, beaten stiff, and whip all together with an egg-beater.

Orange Pudding Sauce

Sweeten half a cup of orange juice with a quarter cup of powdered sugar, and stir till the sugar is dissolved. In a double boiler put four egg yolks and four tablespoons of granulated sugar, beating until it is thick and smooth. Add a heaping teaspoon of cinnamon and, very slowly, the orange juice. Stir for two or three minutes and strain.

Spice Sauce

Mix one tablespoon of cornstarch with one-fourth teaspoon of salt and one-fourth of a cup of water. Add to three-fourths of a cup of boiling water and boil three minutes, stirring constantly. Add one tablespoon of lemon juice and cool. Cream four tablespoons of butter with half a cup of sugar, one-fourth teaspoon each of allspice, cloves and mace, and one-half teaspoon each of ginger and cinnamon. Mix with the cornstarch and fold in the stiffly beaten whites of two eggs.

Cider Sauce

Boil together three-fourths of a cup of maple sugar, two tablespoons of lemon juice and one cup of sweet cider for five minutes.

Lemon Sauce

Mix half a cup of sugar with two tablespoons of cornstarch. Add slowly one cup of boiling water, stirring constantly. Boil five minutes. Remove from fire, and add two tablespoons each of butter and lemon juice.

Maple Sauce for Ice Cream

Take one pound of maple sugar, one cup of thin cream and two tablespoons of butter, and boil till it will form a soft ball in water. Do not stir. Add broken nut meats (preferably butternut) and keep in a pan of hot water till needed.

Honey Sauce for Ice Cream

Chop fine half a cup of butternuts, one-fourth cup of seeded raisins, half a dozen white grapes and a small piece of preserved ginger. Add a cup of strained honey and the juice of half a lemon.

Honey Sauce

Cook together two tablespoons of butter and two teaspoons of cornstarch, being careful not to brown. Add half a cup of honey and one or two tablespoons of water, and cook for a few minutes more.

Brown Sauce

Cream a tablespoon each of flour and butter, and blend with a teaspoon of lemon juice. Cook till brown, add two cups of beef stock, season and thicken.

Cold Meat Sauce

Cook an egg hard, mash the yolk and chop the white. Add to the yolk a teaspoon of sugar, the same of dry mustard, half as much salt, one tablespoon of olive oil and two of vinegar. Mix well and add the chopped white.

Vegetable Sauce

In a double boiler put one whole egg and two yolks, well beaten, and half a cup of sugar. Have the water very hot but not boiling, and stir while adding slowly half a cup of wine. When slightly thick, add a teaspoon of lemon juice, then turn the mixture into a cold dish to arrest the cooking at once.

WHAT MIGHT be called a fundamental Vermont recipe is sour cream biscuit. They are eaten hot for supper with maple syrup, honey or preserves. The same batter is used as the pastry for meat pies of all kinds. It is baked in one large cake and split for shortcakes—strawberry, apple and many others. It is combined with apples for an apple pudding. It is most important and here is the recipe:

Sour Cream Biscuit

Sift together two cups of flour and one teaspoon each of soda, baking powder and salt. Cut this into a cup of thick sour cream, mixing well, and roll out about half an inch thick. Cut with a biscuit cutter, and brush with milk before putting in the oven. Sour milk or buttermilk may be used instead of cream. If this is done, add two tablespoons of shortening, and use a little less than a cup of milk.

Cream Scones

Mix one and a third cups of flour with a little salt, a heaping teaspoon of baking powder and a cup of light cream. Bake as scones, dropping from a spoon on a hot griddle, or as muffins. They can be used in the same way as sour cream biscuit, and are simpler to make and more delicate. They are excellent for tea.

Cornmeal Rolls

Sift together one and one-half cups white flour, three-fourths cup of cornmeal, three teaspoons of baking powder and one of salt. Rub in three tablespoons of butter, add one beaten egg and half a cup of milk. Roll rather thin, cut with biscuit cutter, spread with butter, fold like Parker House rolls and bake quickly.

Crackling Cornbread—Imitation

Beat an egg with one and one-third cups milk. Add two teaspoons white sugar, two tablespoons brown sugar, one-third cup flour, one cup coarse cornmeal, one teaspoon salt and three tablespoons of chopped cooked bacon. Bake in pan greased with bacon fat.

Vermont Johnny Cake

Pour boiling water over cornmeal to a little less than the usual consistency of cornbread batter. Salt and pour very thin in large baking-pan. Pour melted butter over before putting into a hot oven.

Brown Bread

To a cup of sour milk add one-fourth cup of molasses. Stir in a mixture of two cups of cornmeal and one of white or graham flour, to which has been added a teaspoon of soda and half a teaspoon of salt. Steam for about three hours.

Dumplings (1)

Whip an egg, white and yolk separately, mix together and add salt and two tablespoons of water. Mix slowly in white flour to which baking powder has been added in the proportion of a teaspoon to a cup, so the mixture can be handled with a spoon. Drop from a tablespoon dipped in cold water.

Dumplings (2)

Sift together three times two coffee cups of flour, two teaspoons of baking powder and one-half teaspoon of salt. Put the beaten white of an egg in a coffee cup, add four tablespoons of melted butter and fill with milk. Mix with the dry ingredients. Cook fifteen minutes, tightly covered, and without removing cover.

Yorkshire Pudding

Make a rather stiff batter of three eggs, a pint of milk, one teaspoon of salt and two to two and one-half cups of flour. Bake thin.

Dewey Rolls

To one and one-third cups of flour, add two teaspoons of baking powder, one-third of a cup of sugar and half a teaspoon of salt. Add two eggs beaten with half a cup of milk and, lastly, four tablespoons of melted butter. Put in small muffin rings and bake in a quick oven.

Orange Biscuit

Sift together two cups of flour, two teaspoons of baking powder and half a teaspoon of salt. Work in two tablespoons of shortening, and then add a little less than one cup of milk. Roll half an inch thick, cut out and push into the center of each biscuit a lump of sugar moistened in orange juice. Grate orange rind over the tops.

Whole Wheat Muffins

Mix together three cups of whole wheat flour, three teaspoons of baking powder, a teaspoon of salt and two teaspoons of sugar. Work in two tablespoons of butter. Add a beaten egg and one cup each of water and milk.

Bran Muffins

Blend a tablespoon of maple syrup and three tablespoons of butter. Add this to a mixture of one cup of flour and one cup of bran, with a teaspoon of salt and two teaspoons of baking powder. Then add a cup and a half of milk. Beat thoroughly and bake twenty to twenty-five minutes.

Popovers

Mix one and one-fourth cups of flour with one teaspoon of sugar and one-fourth teaspoon of salt. Add gradually a cup of milk and two well-beaten eggs. Beat thoroughly. Have iron rings well greased and very hot, fill about half full and bake from thirty to forty minutes.

Maple Breakfast Rolls

One egg, one half cup each of milk and cream, and three teaspoons granulated maple sugar; add flour, with two teaspoons baking powder and one-half teaspoon salt, till about as thick as griddle cake batter. Bake in muffin tins.

Maple Fritters

Three eggs, one tablespoon sweet cream, one half teaspoon salt, two cups sweet milk, two teaspoons baking powder, about four cups of flour. Mix the baking powder thoroughly with the flour. Add the flour to the milk. Add the salt. Add the eggs, well beaten. Fry in hot lard. Serve hot with warm maple syrup.

IN PUDDINGS, the oldest is probably the boiled Indian pudding—the "bag pudding." There was also the Indian pudding baked. These require too much time, however, and are not often made in these days. The wonderful variety of apples in Vermont accounts for their common use in desserts, and apple roly poly is a great favorite, served with the sweetened cream so often given in old recipes as a pudding sauce. This is the roly poly recipe:

Apple Roly Poly

Make a biscuit dough of two cups of flour, one teaspoon of salt, three teaspoons of baking powder, one cup of milk and two tablespoons of shortening. Roll out about one-fourth of an inch in thickness. Mix half a cup of sugar and a teaspoon of cinnamon, spread over the dough, then cover it with a cup of finely sliced apples. Roll and cut across in two inch slices. Put in baking-pan, sprinkle with sugar and dot generously with butter. Bake for about half an hour. Serve with sweetened cream—cream in which grated maple sugar has been stirred and nutmeg to season.

Honey Custard

Beat five eggs lightly—not to a foam—add half a cup of honey, four cups of scalded milk, one-fourth teaspoon of cinnamon and one-fourth teaspoon of salt. Place custard dishes in a pan of water to bake.

Huckleberry Dumplings

Sift together two cups of flour, two teaspoons of baking powder, and one-half teaspoon of salt. Work into this a tablespoon of lard. Add milk until of the right consistency to roll. Cut out the dumplings an inch thick. Boil a quart of huckleberries with half a pint of water and half a cup of sugar for twenty minutes. Drop in dumplings, cover tightly and boil for twenty minutes.

Brown Betty

Butter a baking-dish and line it with apples sliced fine. Cover with a layer of bread crumbs, sprinkle with maple sugar and cinnamon and dot with butter. Repeat till full. Cover with thick sweetened apple sauce. Bake forty minutes.

Apple Tapioca

Soak three-fourths of a cup of tapioca for one hour in cold water. Drain and add two and one-half cups of boiling water. Cook till transparent. Core and pare seven apples, place them in a baking-dish, filling the cavities with maple sugar. Pour the tapioca over them and bake till the apples are soft. Serve with sweetened cream.

Rice Pudding

Cook a pint of rice in a pint of milk in a double boiler till dry. Then add to the rice one quart of rich milk, four well-beaten eggs, one and one-half cups of seeded raisins, and salt, sugar and cinnamon to taste. Bake forty-five minutes.

Rice Pudding Supreme

Take two cups of hot boiled rice, and add one-fourth box of gelatine dissolved in half a cup of water. Stir till cool, and add a cup of whipped cream, two teaspoons of vanilla and two table-spoons of sugar. Chop three figs and three tablespoons of preserved ginger, and simmer in a syrup made of half a cup of sugar and one-fourth cup of water. Add these to the rice, blend well and put the whole in the ice-box for two hours. Serve with whipped cream, or with sweetened cream from which a seasoning has been omitted.

Strawberry Pudding

One third cup butter, three-quarters of a cup of sugar, one-half cup milk, one and three-quarters cups flour, one egg, two level teaspoons baking powder. Bake in cake tin twenty-five to thirty minutes.

Sauce.—Cream one-third cup butter, add one cup powdered sugar, white of one egg beaten stiff, and lastly two cups fresh strawberries mashed fine.

Snow Pudding

Mix four tablespoons of cornstarch and two tablespoons of sugar with half a cup of cold water. Cook well in a cup and a half of boiling water, take from the fire and salt, add the whites of four eggs, beaten stiff, and a teaspoon of almond extract. Put any kind of fruit in the bottom of a serving-dish, pour mixture over and cool, and serve with fruit juice. The fruit juice may be thickened by adding sugar and cooking for a few moments.

Chocolate Pudding

Place a quart of milk, less half a cup, on the fire in a double boiler. With the cold milk mix three tablespoons of cornstarch. Beat two eggs with half a cup of powdered sugar and half a teaspoon of salt. Mix with the cornstarch and stir into the boiling milk, beating well. Dissolve two ounces of chocolate and four tablespoons of sugar in two tablespoons of boiling water. Beat into the hot pudding and cook for ten minutes from the time the eggs are added.

Bread Pudding

Soak a slice of bread an inch thick in cold water. If slices are small, use more. Drain it, squeeze it dry and crumble. Scald two cups of milk. Add to the milk half a cup of sugar, two tablespoons of butter, one-fourth of a teaspoon of salt and the beaten yolks of two eggs. Season with cloves. Pour over the bread and mix well. Bake till brown.

Cottage Pudding

Cream one-fourth of a cup of butter and half a cup of sugar. Add a beaten egg. Sift two cups flour, three teaspoons baking powder and half a teaspoon of salt. Add alternately with one cup of milk to the first mixture. Bake thirty-five minutes. Serve with lemon sauce.

Puff Pudding

Blend one egg, one tablespoon of sugar, one of butter, four or five of milk, a cup of flour and a heaping teaspoon of baking powder. Place in fireproof cups or large muffin rings two tablespoons of any kind of jam and fill half full of the batter. Bake in a quick oven.

Boiled Indian Pudding

In a quart of boiling milk stir enough cornmeal (mixed with two tablespoons of flour) to make a thick batter. Add one teaspoon of salt, one teaspoon of ginger and half a cup of molasses. Dip the pudding bag in cold water, wring it out and flour the inside. Fill only half full, and boil four to five hours.

Baked Indian Pudding

Boil three pints of milk. Add to it one pint of cornmeal mixed with five tablespoons of flour. When cool, add three well-beaten eggs, two tablespoons of butter, three-fourths cup of sugar, one teaspoon of salt and three of cinnamon. If raisins are added, use one more cup of milk. Bake slowly for two and a half hours.

Apple Pudding

One layer of wheat bread sliced thin, one layer of sliced apples, sprinkled with sugar. Put on another layer of bread and apples and so on alternately until the dish is full. Flavor with lemon. Moisten slightly with water. Cover and bake one-half hour. Serve with maple syrup.

ABOUT THIS matter of eating pie for breakfast of which Vermonters have been accused. It must be admitted that at one time the accusation was justified, and even now pie might be found on the breakfast table in outlying farm districts. It should be realized, however, that there is a great difference between those who rise in the morning, dress and breakfast, and those who rise, put in several hours of heavy farm labor and then breakfast. Anyhow, Vermont has been a great pie state, and it is difficult to select a typical pie from the list. Perhaps the cider apple pie is the most characteristic, and this is the way to make it:

Cider Apple Pie

Pare sweet apples and cut them into eighths. Boil them in cider until the apples are soft and a rich dark red, and the liquid is cooked down to one-fourth of the original amount. If it does not seem thick enough for the filling of a pie, a little flour can be added. Sweeten to taste, spice if desired and bake the pie with one crust, placing strips of pastry across the top.

Green Apple Pie

Make apple sauce of green apples (picked a short time before they are ripe), strain and sweeten. Fill the pie, adding caraway seed, and bake with two crusts. When ready to serve, cut out the top crust carefully, pour in half a cup of thick, sweet cream, stir in lightly and replace the crust.

Dried Apple Pie

Soak the dried apple in water over night, and stew till soft. Mash fine, grate in the peel of half a lemon, and sweeten to taste with maple sugar. Bake with one crust and strips of pastry.

Sarah's Green Mountain Pie

Cut apples in eighths and fill a lower crust. Sprinkle with one cup of sugar mixed with two tablespoons of flour, a little salt and nutmeg or cinnamon. Dot with butter, and pour over half a cup of sweet cream. Place strips of pastry across the top.

Old-Time Pumpkin Pie

Use half a pint of grated pumpkin, uncooked, to a quart of milk. Add three tablespoons of maple sugar, a little salt and two tablespoons of butter. Sift meal on a buttered pie-pan for a crust, about one-fourth of an inch thick, and bake one and one-fourth hours.

Pumpkin Pie Modern

Stew the pumpkin and strain. Take two cups of it, add two cups of milk, three-fourths of a cup of maple sugar, two beaten eggs, one teaspoon of cinnamon, one-fourth teaspoon of ginger and half a teaspoon of salt. Beat together for two minutes. Make it with a bottom crust only. Bake for fifteen minutes in a hot oven, then slowly in moderate heat for forty-five minutes longer.

Rhubarb Pie

Make this with two crusts. Mix one cup of sugar with four cups of diced rhubarb. Add a tablespoon each of lemon juice and butter, and one beaten egg. Dot with butter before adding the top crust.

Peach Pie

Line the pie plate and fill with the halves of peaches, fresh or canned, placing them with the hollow side up. Sprinkle with maple sugar, and pour over enough sour cream to cover. Place strips of pastry on the top.

Custard Pie

Beat together the whites of two eggs and the yolks of four, adding two tablespoons of maple sugar, a little salt and two teaspoons of flour. Add about two cups of milk. After pouring into the crust, sprinkle the custard with nutmeg. Make a meringue, using the two remaining egg whites, beaten very stiff, two tablespoons of white sugar, vanilla and one-fourth of .a teaspoon of cream of tartar.

Lemon Pie

Blend a cup of sugar with a tablespoon of butter, the beaten yolks of two eggs and a rounded tablespoon of flour. Add the juice and grated rind of two lemons and a cup and a half of boiling water. Cook in a double boiler till thick, then fill a baked crust. Use the two egg whites for a meringue.

Raisin Pie

Cook two cups of seeded raisins in a cup and a half of boiling water for five minutes. Mix half a cup of sugar with three table-spoons of flour, dissolve in a little cold water, add to the raisins and cook till thick. Remove from the fire and add a tablespoon each of lemon and orange rind grated, the juice of one orange, two tablespoons of lemon juice and a cup of butternuts chopped. Bake with a top crust.

Cranberry Pie

Cook together for ten minutes one and a half cups of cran-berries, one cup of sugar and two-thirds of a cup of water, break-ing up the berries as they cook. Add two tablespoons of sifted bread crumbs and a little salt. Dot the pie with butter and bake with one crust.

Cranberry and Raisin Pie

Cook together one and one-half cups of cranberries and half a cup of raisins, with one cup of water. Cool, then add three-fourths of a cup of maple sugar and one-half a cup of flour mixed together, and boil for five minutes. Make this pie with two crusts.

Mince Pie

Take one part of beef, well cooked, to two parts of tart apple. Chop fine and mix. Add seeded raisins, whole. Sweeten to taste with maple or muscovado sugar and a little molasses. Add salt, spice with cinnamon and cloves and moisten with cider or brandy. Use two crusts and, before putting on the top crust, dot the mincemeat with butter.

Mince Meat Vermont

Mix one quart of chopped beef, one-half pound of suet, one cup of butter, one pint of molasses, two quarts of chopped apples, two cups of raisins, two pounds of maple sugar, one tablespoon each of cloves, allspice, and cinnamon. Boil slowly in two quarts of sweet cider for two or three hours, being careful not to let it burn.

CAKES

FROM A list of favorite cakes, perhaps a butternut cake is most typical of Vermont. Butternuts are not easy to find outside of New England, though they have the most wonderful flavor and richness of any nut in the world. For use in cookery they are unsurpassed. Probably the fact that they are hard to crack has kept them from popularity, but they should be better known. Maple syrup is also employed in this cake and the recipe is the following:

Butternut Cake

Blend half a cup of butter and half a cup of sugar, then add one cup of maple syrup. Stir in two beaten eggs. Sift together two and one-half cups of flour, two teaspoons of baking powder, three-fourths of a teaspoon of soda and one-half teaspoon of ginger. Add half a cup of hot water. Stir in half a cup of butternut meats. Bake in a loaf and use a frosting made as follows: Two cups of maple sugar and one cup of cream. Boil to the soft ball stage, add a half cup of butternut meats and stir till creamy.

Pound Cake

Cream one pound of butter and one pound of sugar, and add the beaten yolks of seven eggs. Add one pound of flour, then the beaten whites of nine eggs. Add salt and flavoring, and bake in a moderate oven.

Old-Time Cider Cake

Blend three fourths of a pound of sugar and half a pound of butter. Add two teaspoons of soda in half a cup of water, and half a pint of cider. Stir in two pounds of flour and some grated nutmeg. Bake thirty minutes, and eat fresh.

Quick Chocolate Cake

Melt together one and one-half squares of chocolate and three tablespoons of butter. Put in a mixing-bowl with one cup of sugar, half a cup of milk, and one cup of flour sifted with two teaspoons of baking powder and a little salt. Break in two eggs and add one teaspoon of vanilla. Do not stir until all the ingredients have been added, then blend thoroughly with an egg-beater. Bake in a moderate oven.

Layer Cake

Cream half a cup of butter with one and one-half cups sugar, and add the beaten yolks of four eggs. Mix two cups of flour, two teaspoons of baking powder and a little salt, and add alternately with three-fourths cup of milk. Then add one teaspoon of vanilla, and fold in the stiffly beaten whites of the eggs. Bake in three layers, and ice when cold with the maple cream frosting.

Old-Fashioned Layer Cake

Cream one well-beaten egg with a cup of sugar and two table-spoons of butter. Add slowly half a cup of milk, then one and one-half cups of flour and two teaspoons of baking powder. Beat with an egg-beater. Use a lemon filling made as follows: Mix one cup of sugar with two and one-half tablespoons of flour. Add to this the grated rind of two lemons, one-fourth cup of lemon juice and one egg beaten slightly. Put one teaspoon of butter in a saucepan, add the mixture and stir constantly till thick.

Raspberry Tea Cake

Melt a tablespoon of butter and cream it with a cup of sugar. Add two well-beaten eggs, half a teaspoon of salt, a pinch of mace, a cup of milk, and two cups of flour sifted with three tea-spoons of baking powder. Stir till smooth and bake in two layers. Spread with butter and raspberry jam, and serve hot.

Wine Cake

Beat to a cream half a cup of butter with two full cups of powdered sugar. Add the yolks of four eggs, then half a glass of sherry or Madeira, and beat till very light. Add half a cup of cream with a pinch of soda in it, and beat two minutes. Add very quickly the beaten whites of the eggs, three and a half cups of sifted flour, and a little nutmeg.

Maple Sugar Gingerbread

Sift one teaspoon of ginger, one half teaspoon of salt, and one teaspoon of soda with two cups of flour. Mix one beaten egg, one cup of sour cream, and one cup of maple syrup. Combine the two mixtures.

Colonial Gingerbread

Put a cup of New Orleans molasses in a bowl with half a cup of butter and half a cup of sugar. Over this pour a cup of boiling water in which a level dessertspoon of soda has been dissolved. Stir well, and cool. Add a cup each of chopped nut meats and seeded raisins, a teaspoon each of cinnamon and ginger, a teaspoon of salt and two and a half cups of flour. Mix thoroughly, and add two well-beaten eggs. Serve warm.

Honey Cake

Warm and mix one cup of honey and half a cup of butter. Add the yolks of three eggs, unbeaten, and half a teaspoon each of cinnamon and ginger. Mix well. Add three cups of flour and one teaspoon of soda, then the stiffly beaten whites of the three eggs. Add a cup of butternut meats and bake in a loaf.

Peach Cake

Cream four tablespoons of butter and one-fourth of a cup of sugar. Add one beaten egg. Mix with two cups of flour, four teaspoons of baking powder and one teaspoon of salt, adding it to the mixture. Add three-fourths of a cup of milk. Bake in a square pan with sliced peaches on top of the batter.

Seed Cake

Cream two tablespoons of butter, add two tablespoons of sugar and beat for several minutes. Add three eggs, one at a time, beating in thoroughly. Stir in slowly one-half pound of flour and a teaspoon of caraway seeds, with a little salt. Bake for forty minutes.

Maple Sugar Cream Cake

Beat one egg and add to one cup of maple sugar. Stir until the sugar is dissolved. Sift one-half teaspoon of salt and one teaspoon of soda with one and one-half cups of flour. Add to first mixture alternately with one-half cup of sour cream. Bake in a quick oven.

Huckleberry Cake

Cream together two tablespoons of butter and one cup of sugar. Stir in two beaten eggs, then one cup of milk. To two large cups of flour, add two teaspoons of baking powder and one of salt. Sift into fruit and mix well, then add the other ingredients. Bake about forty minutes in a fairly hot oven.

BEVERAGES

Recipes for the beverages of Vermont are too numerous for a complete listing. Almost every kitchen or cellar boasts its own concoctions, either fermented or unfermented. We shall present only a few representative brews, reminding you that there are many variations in the treatment of each.

Beef Tea

Have a pound of prime lean beef—a juicy steak is best—chopped fine by your butcher; put in a chafing dish or double boiler with a cup water, and simmer for several hours, without allowing it to boil. Strain off the juice thoroughly. This stock will keep for some time. Dilute with boiling water to the required strength and season as desired.

Dandelion Wine

One gallon dandelion blossoms gathered while the sun is shining so they will be open, over which pour one gallon water and let stand in a cool place for three days. Then put into a porcelain kettle with the rind of one lemon cut fine and also the rind of three oranges; boil fifteen minutes, then strain. Add the juice of the lemon and oranges, and also the pulp, with three pounds sugar. When lukewarm add one-half yeast cake. Let it stand one week in a warm place, then strain again and let it stand until it stops working, after which bottle.

Flax Seed Lemonade

Into one pint hot water put two tablespoons sugar and three tablespoons whole flax seed. Steep for one hour, then strain. Add juice one lemon and set aside until required.

Grape Shrub

Put sour or wild grapes into a porcelain kettle; cover with water and let come to a boil. Strain and add one-half as much sugar as juice; then boil enough to skim. Bottle and drive corks in securely, having boiled the corks.

Kumyss

One pint milk, one tablespoon white sugar, one-half condensed yeast cake. Dissolve the sugar and yeast cake in a little warm water, fill a patent beer bottle within two inches of the top. In winter leave in a warm room for twelve hours before using, then set away and keep cool. In summer, after twelve hours, put it where it will be cold.

Oatmeal Gruel

Two tablespoons oatmeal boiled one-half hour in one pint milk and one pint water. Strain and pour over one-half teaspoon soda and one small teaspoon salt. Very nourishing and delicious if cold.

Raspberry Vinegar

Spread the berries level in a mixing bowl and cover with vinegar; let them stand twenty-four hours and then strain through a jelly bag. Measure one pound sugar to each pint juice and scald for fifteen minutes. Skim and seal in fruit jars.

Rhubarb Shrub

Cut rhubarb into inch pieces (using pink ends of stalks only). Boil till soft, strain, add juice of one lemon for each quart juice. Sweeten to taste. Bottle and seal. Dilute with ice water when used.

Rhubarb Wine

Twelve quarts rhubarb cut in inch pieces and bruised. Put into twelve quarts water and fifteen pounds sugar. Let stand three days, stirring twice a day. Then strain and put into a cask with one-half ounce isinglass dissolved in a little of the wine. Let it stand two months, then bottle.

Raspberry Wine

Take some fine raspberries, bruise them with the back of a spoon, then strain through a flannel bag into a stone jar; to each quart juice put a pound of double-refined sugar, stir well together and cover it close; let it stand three days, then pour it off clear; to one quart juice put two quarts white wine and bottle it. It will be fit to drink in a week.

Modern Metheglin

To some new honey (that which runs from the comb is best)

add spring water; put in an egg; boil this liquor until the egg swims above the liquor; strain; clear, and pour into a cask. To every fifteen gallons add two ounces of bruised ginger, one ounce cloves and mace, one and one-half ounces cinnamon, all bruised together and tied up in a muslin bag; accelerate the fermentation with yeast; when worked sufficiently bung up; in six weeks draw off into bottles.

Mead

Take eight gallons of water and as much honey as will make it bear an egg (float an egg) ; add to this the rinds of six lemons, and boil it well, scumming it carefully as it rises. When it is off the fire, put to it the juice of the six lemons, and pour it into a clean tub or earthen vessel, if you have one large enough, to work three days; then scum it well, and pour off the clear into the cask, and let it stand open until it has stopped making a hissing noise; after which stop it up close, and in three months' time it will be fine and fit for bottling.

Elderberry Beer

Boil in eighteen gallons of the finest and strongest wort one one-half pecks of elderberries which are quite ripe. Strain clear and when cold work the liquor in the barrel and let it remain there one year, at which time it may be bottled. You may add a few hops and some spices tied in a bag.

Vermont Beer

Take four ounces of hops and boil them in a sufficient quantity of water for three hours. Put the liquor in a clean barrel, and fill it with water after adding two quarts of molasses and a pint of emptings while the liquor is still warm. Let it stand twenty-four hours with the bung out a little, when it will be fit for use. Do it in this manner and it will be good and wholesome beer.

Spruce Beer (1)

To make spruce beer out of the essence, take seven ounces of essence of spruce and fourteen pounds of molasses for an eighteen gallon cask. Mix them with a few gallons of hot water and pour into the cask. Then fill the cask with cold water, stir well, make it about lukewarm, and add two-thirds of a pint of good yeast or the grounds of porter. Let it stand for four or five days to work, then bung it up tight. Two or three days later it will be fit for bottling and immediate use.

Spruce Beer (2)

To make spruce beer out of shed spruce. To one quart of shed spruce add two gallons of cold water, and so on in proportion to the quantity you wish to make. Then add one pint of molasses to every two gallons, let it boil four or five hours and stand until it is lukewarm. Then put one pint of yeast to ten gallons, let it work, and cask it. Bung the cask tight and in two days the beer will be fit for use.

Nettle Beer

Take two pounds of ordinary nettles and boil down in water to a concentrated essence. Now add boiling water to make three gallons. To this add three pounds granulated sugar, the juice and sliced rinds of three lemons, one-half ounce ground ginger and one tablespoonful of cream of tartar. Let stand until lukewarm and then add one yeast cake dissolved in warm water and keep this mixture in a crock until fermentation causes head or foam. Skim off head and bottle. Fermentation will take place within twenty-four hours if crock is set in warm room 65-70. This beer will be ready to drink in two or three days.

Vermont Ginger Beer

Two lemons should first be peeled, after which squeeze out and strain the juice of the lemons. Then put one and one-half pounds bruised ginger, two and one-half pounds loaf sugar, one ounce cream of tartar and the rind and juice of the lemons into an earthen crock. On these various ingredients pour three gallons boiling water. When this is almost cool add two yeast cakes. This should now be thoroughly stirred, and then placed, covered, in a warm place, as beside a stove. The following day skim off the surface of the liquid, and syphon into bottles, taking care not to disturb the yeasty sediment. The beer will be ready for use in three days. Ginger beer should be made only during the summer months.

Grandfather's Nightcap

Beat the yolk one egg with one teaspoon allspice and one gill rum, melt one teaspoon sugar in one cup boiling water. Whisk this well and stir; strain into a hot glass, placing the beaten white on top; dust with nutmeg.

ASKING A long-exiled Vermonter—"What do you remember liking best to eat when you were a child?"—the answer was: "Bread and milk and baked sweet apples." One could hardly imagine a more simple and unsophisticated repast. But it had a very special and delicious flavor. The apples were really sweet apples, not just mild, and were baked slowly with a little water and maple syrup. They were cut in pieces and added to the bread and milk.

Maple Sugar on Snow

Either sugar or syrup may be used, but the syrup, if obtainable, is best. Boil the syrup until, when dropped on snow, it remains on the surface and becomes waxy. Then spread it upon the surface of the snow or a block of ice. If the sugar is used, add a little water and melt it, being careful not to burn, and treat in same manner as the syrup. If served in the middle of a maple grove, when the air is rich with spring aromas, and the ground moist with melting snow, this dish is without equal. If you lack a maple grove, it is still a delicacy even when served indoors.

Honey Cookies

To one and one-half cups of honey and one cup of sugar, add one-half cup of citron, shredded, one cup of butternut meats, chopped, one teaspoon of cinnamon and one-half teaspoon of salt. Add enough flour to make a soft dough.

Raisin Cookies

Mix one beaten egg, one and one-half cups of sugar, and half a cup each of milk and melted butter. Add flour to roll easily, the flour sifted with two teaspoons of baking powder and one-fourth teaspoon of salt. Roll out and cut thin, putting two together with this mixture between: One cup of chopped raisins, half a cup of sugar, half a cup of water, one heaping teaspoon of flour and a little nutmeg.

Old-Time Gingersnaps

Boil one cup of molasses for five minutes. Remove and add one-half cup of butter and one teaspoon each of soda and ginger. Cool, stir in flour till thick enough to roll, then roll out as thin as possible. Bake in a hot oven.

Baked Bananas

Put bananas in a baking-dish, slitting the skin on the top and folding back from the fruit. Make a syrup of a cup of water, half a cup of sugar, maple or brown, a tablespoon each of orange and lemon juice and one of butter. Pour over and bake twenty-five minutes, basting with the syrup.

Apples in Maple Syrup

Cut eight apples in halves, remove cores and put in baking-dish, flat side up, with one cup of maple syrup, two tablespoons of butter and one and one-half cups water. Bake till the apples are soft and the syrup thick, basting occasionally.

Baked Apples

Core half a dozen apples and pare one-third of the way down. Put them in a saucepan with a cup of brown or maple sugar and two cups of water. Cover close and cook till soft. Then place in a baking-dish, pour the syrup over them and bake till brown. When serving, place apple jelly in the cavities.

Figs in Cider

Cut the figs in two or three pieces, cover with sweet cider and let them stand over night. Simmer very slowly, covered, till the figs are soft and the cider has thickened to a rich sauce. Add sugar if necessary, and serve with whipped cream.

Jam Pancakes

Boil together for ten minutes two tablespoons of butter, two teaspoons of sugar, the grated rind of a lemon and a cup of water. Stir in till smooth three-fourths of a cup of flour, remove from fire and beat in thoroughly five eggs, one at a time. Cool, then roll the dough very thin. Cut in rounds, and put two rounds together with a filling of any kind of jam or marmalade. Pinch the edges together, fry brown in butter and serve hot, dusted with sugar.

Cottage Cheese

Put thick sour milk in a pan and place on the stove where it will heat very slowly till it wheys, being careful not to let it get tough. Drain through a cloth, add melted butter and cream, and season with salt and caraway seeds. Sage is also good as a seasoning.

Doughnuts

Cream a cup of sugar with two tablespoons melted butter. Add two beaten eggs and one cup of milk. To three and a half cups sifted flour add three teaspoons baking powder, half a teaspoon of salt and nutmeg or cinnamon, adding to the other ingredients. Fry in hot fat.

Seed Cakes

Cream two cups of sugar with one cup of butter, and add three tablespoons of milk. Sift two cups of flour with one and one-half teaspoons of baking powder and half a teaspoon of salt, and add. Stir in two tablespoons of caraway seeds.

Maple Sweet Pickles

Seven pounds of fruit, one pint best maple or cider vinegar, one tablespoon ground cinnamon, three pounds of maple sugar, one teaspoon ground cloves, one teaspoon ground allspice. Boil until the fruit is tender. This is excellent for plums, pears, peaches, or cucumbers.

A LIST OF SUGGESTIONS FOR VARIETY

Two or three cloves in cream of tomato soup—and in tea.

Grated cheese on baked fish.

One-fourth teaspoon of baking powder in icing, souffles and mashed potato.

Hamburg steak moistened, sprinkled with minced onion and baked.

Minced nasturtium, mint or sorrel in omelet and creamed potatoes.

Cooked carrots put through a ricer.

Spinach seasoned with nutmeg.

Chopped mint added to peas.

Potatoes dipped in flour for frying.

Butter or olive oil brushed over potatoes for baking.

Sorrel added to green salads.

Caraway seeds in cottage cheese or in cream cheese for sandwiches.

Cheese grated on apple pie and melted in oven before serving.

Tapioca or rice pudding covered with marshmallows and browned.

Caraway seeds in applesauce or apple pie.

Rice cooked in milk—just enough to cook dry, as rice is tender.

Marshmallow in bottom of custard cups.

Grated chocolate or cinnamon added to whipped cream.

Cream or milk on honey.

One-fourth teaspoon of cream of tartar in meringues.

Honey on sliced tomatoes.

Pinch of salt in coffee when making.

INDEX

Miscellaneous

Puddings

Soups

Vegetables

A CATALOGUE OF SELECTED DOVER BOOKS
IN ALL FIELDS OF INTEREST

A CATALOGUE OF SELECTED DOVER BOOKS
IN ALL FIELDS OF INTEREST

THE NOTEBOOKS OF LEONARDO DA VINCI, edited by J.P. Richter. Extracts from manuscripts reveal great genius; on painting, sculpture, anatomy, sciences, geography, etc. Both Italian and English. 186 ms. pages reproduced, plus 500 additional drawings, including studies for Last Supper, Sforza monument, etc. 860pp. 7⅞ x 10¾.   USO 22572-0, 22573-9 Pa., Two vol. set $15.90

ART NOUVEAU DESIGNS IN COLOR, Alphonse Mucha, Maurice Verneuil, Georges Auriol. Full-color reproduction of Combinaisons ornamentales (c. 1900) by Art Nouveau masters. Floral, animal, geometric, interlacings, swashes — borders, frames, spots — all incredibly beautiful. 60 plates, hundreds of designs. 9⅜ x 8¹/₁₆ .   22885-1 Pa. $4.00

GRAPHIC WORKS OF ODILON REDON. All great fantastic lithographs, etchings, engravings, drawings, 209 in all. Monsters, Huysmans, still life work, etc. Introduction by Alfred Werner. 209pp. 9⅛ x 12¼.   21996-8 Pa. $6.00

EXOTIC FLORAL PATTERNS IN COLOR, E.-A. Seguy. Incredibly beautiful full-color pochoir work by great French designer of 20's. Complete Bouquets et frondaisons, Suggestions pour étoffes. Richness must be seen to be believed. 40 plates containing 120 patterns. 80pp. 9⅜ x 12¼.   23041-4 Pa. $6.00

SELECTED ETCHINGS OF JAMES A. McN. WHISTLER, James A. McN. Whistler. 149 outstanding etchings by the great American artist, including selections from the Thames set and two Venice sets, the complete French set, and many individual prints. Introduction and explanatory note on each print by Maria Naylor. 157pp. 9⅜ x 12¼.   23194-1 Pa. $5.00

VISUAL ILLUSIONS: THEIR CAUSES, CHARACTERISTICS, AND APPLICATIONS, Matthew Luckiesh. Thorough description, discussion; shape and size, color, motion; natural illusion. Uses in art and industry. 100 illustrations. 252pp.
21530-X Pa. $3.00

TEN BOOKS ON ARCHITECTURE, Vitruvius. The most important book ever written on architecture. Early Roman aesthetics, technology, classical orders, site selection, all other aspects. Stands behind everything since. Morgan translation. 331pp.
20645-9 Pa. $3.75

THE CODEX NUTTALL, A PICTURE MANUSCRIPT FROM ANCIENT MEXICO, as first edited by Zelia Nuttall. Only inexpensive edition, in full color, of a pre-Columbian Mexican (Mixtec) book. 88 color plates show kings, gods, heroes, temples, sacrifices. New explanatory, historical introduction by Arthur G. Miller. 96pp. 11⅜ x 8½.   23168-2 Pa. $7.50

HOUDINI ON MAGIC, Harold Houdini. Edited by Walter Gibson, Morris N. Young. How he escaped; exposés of fake spiritualists; instructions for eye-catching tricks; other fascinating material by and about greatest magician. 155 illustrations. 280pp. 20384-0 Pa. $2.75

HANDBOOK OF THE NUTRITIONAL CONTENTS OF FOOD, U.S. Dept. of Agriculture. Largest, most detailed source of food nutrition information ever prepared. Two mammoth tables: one measuring nutrients in 100 grams of edible portion; the other, in edible portion of 1 pound as purchased. Originally titled Composition of Foods. 190pp. 9 x 12. 21342-0 Pa. $4.00

COMPLETE GUIDE TO HOME CANNING, PRESERVING AND FREEZING, U.S. Dept. of Agriculture. Seven basic manuals with full instructions for jams and jellies; pickles and relishes; canning fruits, vegetables, meat; freezing anything. Really good recipes, exact instructions for optimal results. Save a fortune in food. 156 illustrations. 214pp. 6⅛ x 9¼. 22911-4 Pa. $2.50

THE BREAD TRAY, Louis P. De Gouy. Nearly every bread the cook could buy or make: bread sticks of Italy, fruit breads of Greece, glazed rolls of Vienna, everything from corn pone to croissants. Over 500 recipes altogether. including buns, rolls, muffins, scones, and more. 463pp. 23000-7 Pa. $4.00

CREATIVE HAMBURGER COOKERY, Louis P. De Gouy. 182 unusual recipes for casseroles, meat loaves and hamburgers that turn inexpensive ground meat into memorable main dishes: Arizona chili burgers, burger tamale pie, burger stew, burger corn loaf, burger wine loaf, and more. 120pp. 23001-5 Pa. $1.75

LONG ISLAND SEAFOOD COOKBOOK, J. George Frederick and Jean Joyce. Probably the best American seafood cookbook. Hundreds of recipes. 40 gourmet sauces, 123 recipes using oysters alone! All varieties of fish and seafood amply represented. 324pp. 22677-8 Pa. $3.50

THE EPICUREAN: A COMPLETE TREATISE OF ANALYTICAL AND PRACTICAL STUDIES IN THE CULINARY ART, Charles Ranhofer. Great modern classic. 3,500 recipes from master chef of Delmonico's, turn-of-the-century America's best restaurant. Also explained, many techniques known only to professional chefs. 775 illustrations. 1183pp. 6⅝ x 10. 22680-8 Clothbd. $22.50

THE AMERICAN WINE COOK BOOK, Ted Hatch. Over 700 recipes: old favorites livened up with wine plus many more: Czech fish soup, quince soup, sauce Perigueux, shrimp shortcake, filets Stroganoff, cordon bleu goulash, jambonneau, wine fruit cake, more. 314pp. 22796-0 Pa. $2.50

DELICIOUS VEGETARIAN COOKING, Ivan Baker. Close to 500 delicious and varied recipes: soups, main course dishes (pea, bean, lentil, cheese, vegetable, pasta, and egg dishes), savories, stews, whole-wheat breads and cakes, more. 168pp. USO 22834-7 Pa. $2.00

VISUAL ILLUSIONS: THEIR CAUSES, CHARACTERISTICS, AND APPLICATIONS, Matthew Luckiesh. Thorough description and discussion of optical illusion, geometric and perspective, particularly; size and shape distortions, illusions of color, of motion; natural illusions; use of illusion in art and magic, industry, etc. Most useful today with op art, also for classical art. Scores of effects illustrated. Introduction by William H. Ittleson. 100 illustrations. xxi + 252pp.

21530-X Paperbound $2.50

A HANDBOOK OF ANATOMY FOR ART STUDENTS, Arthur Thomson. Thorough, virtually exhaustive coverage of skeletal structure, musculature, etc. Full text, supplemented by anatomical diagrams and drawings and by photographs of undraped figures. Unique in its comparison of male and female forms, pointing out differences of contour, texture, form. 211 figures, 40 drawings, 86 photographs. xx + 459pp. 5⅜ x 8⅜.

21163-0 Paperbound $5.00

150 MASTERPIECES OF DRAWING, Selected by Anthony Toney. Full page reproductions of drawings from the early 16th to the end of the 18th century, all beautifully reproduced: Rembrandt, Michelangelo, Dürer, Fragonard, Urs, Graf, Wouwerman, many others. First-rate browsing book, model book for artists. xviii + 150pp. 8⅜ x 11¼.

21032-4 Paperbound $4.00

THE LATER WORK OF AUBREY BEARDSLEY, Aubrey Beardsley. Exotic, erotic, ironic masterpieces in full maturity: Comedy Ballet, Venus and Tannhauser, Pierrot, Lysistrata, Rape of the Lock, Savoy material, Ali Baba, Volpone, etc. This material revolutionized the art world, and is still powerful, fresh, brilliant. With *The Early Work*, all Beardsley's finest work. 174 plates, 2 in color. xiv + 176pp. 8⅛ x 11.

21817-1 Paperbound $4.00

DRAWINGS OF REMBRANDT, Rembrandt van Rijn. Complete reproduction of fabulously rare edition by Lippmann and Hofstede de Groot, completely reedited, updated, improved by Prof. Seymour Slive, Fogg Museum. Portraits, Biblical sketches, landscapes, Oriental types, nudes, episodes from classical mythology—All Rembrandt's fertile genius. Also selection of drawings by his pupils and followers. "Stunning volumes," *Saturday Review*. 550 illustrations. lxxviii + 552pp. 9⅛ x 12¼.

21485-0, 21486-9 Two volumes, Paperbound $12.00

THE DISASTERS OF WAR, Francisco Goya. One of the masterpieces of Western civilization—83 etchings that record Goya's shattering, bitter reaction to the Napoleonic war that swept through Spain after the insurrection of 1808 and to war in general. Reprint of the first edition, with three additional plates from Boston's Museum of Fine Arts. All plates facsimile size. Introduction by Philip Hofer, Fogg Museum. v + 97pp. 9⅜ x 8¼.

21872-4 Paperbound $3.00

GRAPHIC WORKS OF ODILON REDON. Largest collection of Redon's graphic works ever assembled: 172 lithographs, 28 etchings and engravings, 9 drawings. These include some of his most famous works. All the plates from *Odilon Redon: oeuvre graphique complet*, plus additional plates. New introduction and caption translations by Alfred Werner. 209 illustrations. xxvii + 209pp. 9⅛ x 12¼.

21966-8 Paperbound $6.00

COOKIES FROM MANY LANDS, Josephine Perry. Crullers, oatmeal cookies, chaux au chocolate, English tea cakes, mandel kuchen, Sacher torte, Danish puff pastry, Swedish cookies — a mouth-watering collection of 223 recipes. 157pp.
22832-0 Pa. $2.25

ROSE RECIPES, Eleanour S. Rohde. How to make sauces, jellies, tarts, salads, pot-pourris, sweet bags, pomanders, perfumes from garden roses; all exact recipes. Century old favorites. 95pp.
22957-2 Pa. $1.75

"OSCAR" OF THE WALDORF'S COOKBOOK, Oscar Tschirky. Famous American chef reveals 3455 recipes that made Waldorf great; cream of French, German, American cooking, in all categories. Full instructions, easy home use. 1896 edition. 907pp. 6⅝ x 9⅜.
20790-0 Clothbd. $15.00

JAMS AND JELLIES, May Byron. Over 500 old-time recipes for delicious jams, jellies. marmalades, preserves, and many other items. Probably the largest jam and jelly book in print. Originally titled May Byron's Jam Book. 276pp.
USO 23130-5 Pa. $3.50

MUSHROOM RECIPES, André L. Simon. 110 recipes for everyday and special cooking. Champignons à la grecque, sole bonne femme, chicken liver croustades, more; 9 basic sauces, 13 ways of cooking mushrooms. 54pp.
USO 20913-X Pa. $1.25

THE BUCKEYE COOKBOOK, Buckeye Publishing Company. Over 1,000 easy-to-follow, traditional recipes from the American Midwest: bread (100 recipes alone), meat, game, jam, candy, cake, ice cream, and many other categories of cooking. 64 illustrations. From 1883 enlarged edition. 416pp.
23218-2 Pa. $4.00

TWENTY-TWO AUTHENTIC BANQUETS FROM INDIA, Robert H. Christie. Complete, easy-to-do recipes for almost 200 authentic Indian dishes assembled in 22 banquets. Arranged by region. Selected from Banquets of the Nations. 192pp.
23200-X Pa. $2.50